GLADIATORS

by Paul Hoblin

Content Consultant
Laurie J. Churchill, PhD
New Mexico State University

CORE
LIBRARY

Published by ABDO Publishing Company, PO Box 398166, Minneapolis, MN 55439. Copyright © 2013 by Abdo Consulting Group, Inc. International copyrights reserved in all countries. No part of this book may be reproduced in any form without written permission from the publisher. The Core Library™ is a trademark and logo of ABDO Publishing Company.

Printed in the United States of America,
North Mankato, Minnesota
102012
012013

Editor: Lauren Coss
Series Designer: Becky Daum

Cataloging-in-Publication Data
Hoblin, Paul.
 Gladiators / Paul Hoblin.
   p. cm. -- (Great warriors)
Includes bibliographical references and index.
ISBN 978-1-61783-722-7
1. Gladiators--Rome--Juvenile literature. 2. Gladiators--History--Juvenile literature. I. Title.
796.80937--dc22
                                        2012946376

Photo Credits: North Wind/North Wind Picture Archives, cover, 1, 12, 21; Plinio Lepri/AP Images, 4; Thinkstock, 6; Getty Images/Thinkstock, 9, 45; Roger Payne/Getty Images, 10; Red Line Editorial, 13; Time & Life Pictures/Getty Images, 16; Getty Images/Photos.com/Thinkstock, 18, 36; Mansell/Time Life Pictures/Getty Image, 24; Ronald Zak/AP Images, 26; Eric Vandeville/Gamma-Rapho/Getty Images, 28; DEA /A. de Gregorario/ De Agostini/Getty Images, 30; Dorling Kindersley, 32; Bettmann/Corbis/ AP Images, 34; Simon Smith/Shutterstock Images, 38; Murray Close/ Lionsgate/Everett Collection, 40

CONTENTS

CHAPTER ONE

ANCIENT ROME

The entertainment began in the morning. Dozens of humans and animals faced off against one another in the arena. They were part of an animal hunt called the *venatio*. A huge audience cheered them on. The venatio featured lions, elephants, rhinoceroses, gazelles, bulls, and bears. Humans and animals alike fought fiercely to stay alive.

Gladiators were some of the toughest warriors of the Roman empire.

The Colosseum in Rome was built between 70 and 80 CE. It held more than 50,000 spectators. And it still stands today. Take a close look at the image of the Colosseum's ruins above. What do these ruins tell you about the atmosphere of the gladiator games? What might it be like to fight in the Colosseum? How does this image add to your understanding of the gladiator games?

By the afternoon, it was time for the main event. Now there were only two fighters. These weren't just any fighters. These men were gladiators. Both had spent months training for this very moment. Both were experts with their weapons. Each gladiator had fans in the stands.

The fans screamed and cheered as the two fighters traded blows. The crowd applauded when one of the gladiators thrust his sword at his rival. When the other ran away, the crowd shouted angrily. They didn't want to see a chase. They wanted a fight.

The gladiators kicked up clouds of dust as they attacked one another. This was a life-and-death fight for the gladiators. But to everyone else, it was a show.

Finally one of the gladiators stumbled. He fell to the ground. He found the other gladiator's trident pointed at his chest. The fallen gladiator had tossed aside his shield long ago. He had needed to run faster. Now he tossed aside his sword too. He had been beaten. And he knew it.

He only had one more chance to live. He raised his index finger toward the referee. The gladiator was asking the referee for mercy. The referee looked to the crowd. The audience must have admired the way the gladiator had fought. Members of the audience pointed their thumbs toward the ground. This meant they were showing pity to the loser. Still, the final decision wasn't the audience's. It was the emperor's. He was the one who decided whether a losing gladiator would live or die.

This time the emperor listened to the crowd. The gladiator lived. But he was lucky. Gladiators fought in Rome for hundreds of years. The crowd and the emperor often chose differently.

Thumbs-Up or Thumbs-Down?

Most movies about gladiators show the crowd and the emperor giving a thumbs-up gesture to spare a losing gladiator's life. Historians believe the reverse actually happened. When crowd members pointed their thumbs to the ground, they wanted the gladiator to live. If they pointed their thumbs over their shoulders, the gladiator was probably doomed.

When the crowd pointed their thumbs down, it was a signal for the winner to drop his sword. The audience wanted the loser to live.

9

CHAPTER TWO

THE BEGINNINGS OF GLADIATORS

The history of the gladiator is much older than the Roman Empire. The Romans' idea for one-on-one combat came from an ancient people known as the Etruscans. The Etruscans amused themselves at festivals and even private dinner parties by watching men fight to the death.

Gladiator games were an important part of ancient Roman culture.

Augustus was the first of many emperors of the Roman Empire.

The Romans Take Over

Rome began as a republic ruled by elected officials as early as 500 BCE. During this time, the city conquered the rest of the Italian peninsula. The Etruscans were just one of many civilizations the Roman Empire conquered. In the first century BCE, the Romans switched from a republic to an empire.

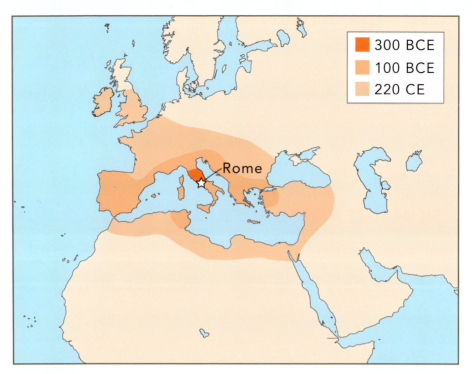

The Roman Empire

The Romans were one of the greatest empires of the ancient world. This map shows their military expansion in 300 BCE, 100 BCE, and 220 CE. What do you think were the reasons for the changes between these years? What can you learn from the rest of this book to help answer the question?

In 27 BCE, Augustus became the first official emperor of the Roman Empire. Emperors ruled Rome and its territories until the fall of the Roman Empire in 476 CE. Each emperor tried to expand Rome's territory. War was nearly constant along the empire's borders.

The Roman Empire was the largest empire in the world for more than 400 years. In the 100s BCE, when the Roman Empire was at its peak, one in four people on Earth lived under its rule.

Fighting at Funerals

The Romans took many prisoners as they conquered first their neighbors and later far-flung lands. Many prisoners were sold into slavery. Others were executed. But some of these prisoners played an important role in Roman funerals. Romans believed that killing a prisoner at a Roman funeral would help the dead Roman move to the world of the dead. In the 200s BCE, gladiator fights began appearing at Roman funerals. The gladiator fights at funerals were a way for

Funeral Fights

The first known funeral to feature gladiators was held in 264 BCE. The sons of Roman Junius Brutus matched three pairs of gladiators against each other to honor their father. The gladiators fought until one man from each pair was dead. Julius Caesar's funeral in 44 BCE featured 300 pairs of gladiators.

many Romans to be entertained while honoring the deceased person at the same time.

Public Entertainment

Gladiators may have fought only at family-sponsored funerals during this time. But there were many forms of public entertainment for Roman audiences. Romans crowded into arenas to watch plays. Romans also loved watching chariot races. Riders in small chariots pulled by four horses raced around an arena at full speed. The sport was dangerous. Many riders were trampled and killed. But the Roman crowd didn't mind the violence.

Another popular form of public entertainment was equally violent: the venatio. By 100 BCE, the Roman Empire stretched into Africa. This meant

The Venatio

A venatio wasn't a true hunt. The animals were confined to the arena. The hunters had no difficulty finding them. And many of the animals ended up hunting the humans. Both humans and animals attacked each other. The event ended when all the animals and many of the humans had been killed.

During the venatio, audiences watched as people in the arena hunted and killed wild animals.

the Romans could ship all kinds of exotic animals back to Italy. They brought elephants, rhinoceroses, lions, and panthers. At first Romans simply paraded these animals through the arena for audiences to look at. But before long the crowds grew bored. Soon people began hunting the animals in the arena.

Introducing the Gladiators

Roman audiences' desire for drama and violence continued growing. The chariot races were thrilling. But audiences wanted more thrills. The animal hunts were intense. But Romans wanted something even more intense. In the middle of the first century BCE, gladiators stepped into the arena.

EXPLORE ONLINE

This chapter focuses on the history of ancient Rome and the gladiator games. Life was very different 2,000 years ago. But Roman life had some things in common with modern life today. Check out the Web site below to learn more about the ancient Romans. How were the Romans similar to you and your family? How was their lifestyle different from how you live? How does the information from the Web site help you understand the chapter better?

Ancient Romans
www.kidspast.com/world-history/0076-ancient-rome.php

WHO WERE THE GLADIATORS?

When the gladiator fights first moved into arenas in the mid-100s BCE, most of the gladiators were prisoners of war. The many captives of Rome's wars became slaves. Their children were also slaves. Soon Romans began using slaves as gladiators. These were often slaves who had committed some type of crime such as theft

Most gladiators were slaves or prisoners of war.

or murder. They were sent to gladiator school as punishment.

This punishment was tough. Gladiator fights were vicious and bloody. Not many gladiators made it out of the arena alive. But being sent to gladiator school was better than being executed. A gladiator had some hope of survival. Some gladiators were even able to buy their way back into society as free men.

Spartacus

People who chose to flee from the Roman army could also find themselves in the arena. Spartacus was a Roman soldier who was caught trying to run away from the army. He was sent to a gladiator training school as punishment. In 73 BCE, he was one of 80 gladiators who escaped the school. Other Roman slaves soon joined Spartacus's group. He led this group of rebels across Italy. They fought the Roman army for two years. Eventually the Roman army caught and killed Spartacus and his followers.

Free Men

Not all men who became gladiators had been forced into the arena. Some free men chose to give up their freedom to become gladiators.

Spartacus became a legend who inspired slaves across the Roman Empire.

Usually they did so to earn money. Men were paid a fee when they agreed to be a gladiator. If successful, they were also paid for their wins. But free men who became gladiators gave up their social status. Successful gladiators might be heroes in the arena. But all gladiators had the social status of a slave.

Emperors in the Arena

Some of Rome's emperors became gladiators as well. However, these leaders weren't real gladiators. Their fights were rigged so that they could not lose.

The emperors had no risk of dying. The men they fought were given swords made of wood. These were no match for the emperor's real weapons. The gladiators were almost certainly required to be careful with these fake weapons. To wound an emperor would likely have meant certain death. The emperors may have been in no danger of dying, but that didn't stop them from killing others.

Female Gladiators

Most gladiators were men. But in the first century CE, many Roman audiences enjoyed watching female gladiators face off in the arena. A stone carving in the British Museum of London, England, shows two of these female gladiators, Amazone and Achillia. Text above the engraving explains that both women were allowed to live. This kind of mercy didn't happen often. It meant the audience and the emperor were impressed by each gladiator's courage and skill.

The Romans may have been disgusted by their emperor's actions. But they couldn't say so. An emperor had the power to order any one of them into the arena if they spoke out.

FURTHER EVIDENCE

Chapter Three covers who gladiators were. What was one of the chapter's main points? What are some pieces of evidence in the chapter that support this main point? Check out the Web site at the link below. Does the information on this Web site support the main point in this chapter? Write a few sentences using new information from the Web site as evidence to support the main point in this chapter.

History for Kids
www.historyforkids.org/learn/romans/games/circus.htm

CHAPTER FOUR

A GLADIATOR'S LIFE

Every person who wanted to become a gladiator was forced to swear an oath. He promised to serve as a gladiator until he was killed or released. A few gladiators earned enough money to purchase their freedom. Occasionally, gladiators were freed after enough success in the arena.

Learning the skills to survive a gladiator fight took a lot of training.

In 2011 archaeologists discovered the ruins of a huge gladiator school buried in Austria. They used technology to scan the site and create a model of the school.

Free men who volunteered to become gladiators also signed a contract. The contract included how much money they would receive and how often they would fight. Those who signed the contract were giving up all of their rights. After a specific amount of time, they could rejoin society. Until that time, the gladiators belonged to the gladiator training school. Most historians believe there were more than 100 gladiator schools. The four most important schools were near the Colosseum in Rome.

Life as a Gladiator

Gladiators were locked up in two-person cells when they weren't training. These cells were small. Most were about 10 feet by 13 feet (3 m by 4 m). Gladiators ate their meals together. Audiences wanted to see a good fight. So gladiators ate food that would help keep them strong.

Gladiators spent most of their days training. New recruits were assigned to a specialist. This specialist would help them master a specific fighting style. These specialists were usually experienced gladiators.

Lean, Mean, Fighting Machines?

Most people imagine gladiators as muscular and lean. Gladiators were certainly strong. But they likely weren't slim. Gladiator schools intentionally fattened up their fighters. A layer of fat could protect the gladiator in the ring. It could also make him more entertaining to watch. Gladiators with more flesh were more likely to get wounds that looked dramatic. This pleased the crowd but allowed the gladiators to continue fighting.

Gladiators in training learned how to use many different kinds of weapons at gladiator schools.

The training grounds were smaller versions of actual gladiator arenas. They were oval shaped. They included poles that the gladiators could practice fighting moves on. A gladiator practiced fighting the pole with a wooden weapon. This exercise improved the gladiator's technique. It also increased his strength and stamina. Other gladiators trained with weighted weapons. If a gladiator used an extra-heavy sword while training, his real sword would feel light when he fought in the arena.

Gladiator schools could be dangerous places. Many fighters in a school were also violent criminals. Almost none of them had any hope for survival. The fear of rebellion was constant. Weapons were locked away whenever they weren't being used. A guard was assigned to watch the weapons at all times.

Killing a Neighbor

Most gladiators would have to kill, or be killed by, someone they knew well. The gladiators who fought against each other were often from the same school. They ate together, lived together, and trained together every day. It was possible that a gladiator could both kill someone and attend his funeral.

Even though people knew how dangerous the schools were, they couldn't help being attracted to the gladiators. Fans often sat in the stands surrounding the training grounds. Emperors even visited the schools to watch the gladiators work out. Watching gladiators practice was the next best thing to watching the actual fights.

CHAPTER FIVE

IN THE ARENA

Gladiator games were about thrilling an audience. The crowd's enjoyment was much more important than the gladiators' safety. Gladiators commonly wore bright colors, brilliant plumes, and beautiful metals. The best gladiators entered the arena decked out in copper, silver, and even gold. But this armor failed to cover all of a gladiator's body. An invincible fighter was no fun to

Gladiators were entertainers, not soldiers.

Gladiators' armor was usually light. Most gladiators wore a shoulder guard called a *galerus*.

watch. The armor was meant to extend a gladiator's life, not to save it.

Different gladiators adopted different fighting styles. The gladiators' armor and weapons were based on these styles. The fighting styles were inspired by fighting techniques in different regions the Romans conquered. But most gladiators didn't fight in the style of their home region. Two opponents fighting each other in the same style was very rare. It was more entertaining to see different kinds of gladiators competing against one another.

Types of Gladiators

A *Thracian* gladiator had a round shield and a curved sword. He wore no armor, except for a helmet. This helmet had a griffin at the top.

Mirmillones were also armed with a sword and a shield. They were often paired against Thracians. Mirmillones' helmets featured tall fins.

A *retiarius* was a gladiator who wore no armor. He fought with a net and a trident. The net was attached to the retiarius's wrist with a leather strap. He also had a dagger in his belt. His goal was to throw the net on top of his rival. He would then attack the trapped opponent with his trident. Because of his lack of armor, a retiarius had to be fast and agile.

Finders Keepers

The Roman Empire conquered many nations. They often saved or copied the conquered nations' armor and weapons. Then they gave it to the gladiators. A Thracian gladiator used the same gear actual Thracians in Thrace, part of modern Turkey, once used.

Retiarius gladiators, right, often fought against secutor gladiators, left.

Secutor gladiators chased their opponents around the arena. A secutor was usually paired with a retiarius. The retiarius would run away while the secutor chased after him.

Roman audiences had complicated views on the gladiators. Tertullian was a Christian man who lived in the Roman Empire during the 100s and 200s CE. In his essay *De Spectaculis*, or "On the Spectacles," he describes the crowd's treatment of the gladiators:

> *During one and the same performance they sing their praises and humiliate and belittle them. They condemn them to public disgrace and to the loss of their rights as citizens. They exclude them from the senate and ban them from the tribunes and from the ranks of senators and knights. They deny them any honor or distinction. . . . But at the same time they love those they punish and disparage those they respect. They hold the skill itself in high regard but despise the man who displays it.*

> Source: Fik Meijer. The Gladiators: History's Most Deadly Sport. New York: Thomas Dunne, 2003. Print. 42.

What's the Big Idea?

Read Tertullian's quote again carefully. What is its main idea? What details in the passage support Tertullian's main idea? Come up with a few sentences calling out two or three supporting details. Explain how they support the main idea.

CHAPTER SIX

GLADIATORS LIVE ON

The Roman Empire began to change as it grew. In 306 CE, Constantine became emperor. Constantine was the first Roman emperor to convert to Christianity. The violence of the gladiator games went against Constantine's Christian beliefs.

In 325 CE, Constantine banned the gladiator games. However, not all Romans were Christians. Most people ignored the ban. Roman audiences

Gladiator games were an important form of entertainment for Romans. But the popularity of the games would not last forever.

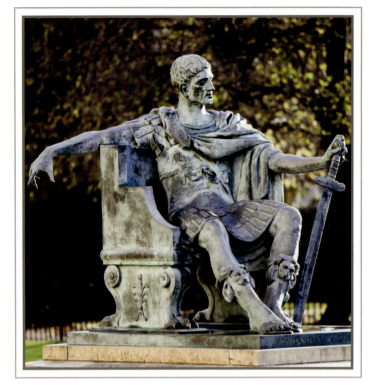

Emperor Constantine encouraged Christianity across the Roman Empire. But the religion did not support the violence of gladiator games.

continued demanding the games. Gladiator fights continued. But they began taking place less often. In 399 CE, the last gladiator school was finally shut down. Gladiator combat is mentioned in writings from as late as the 440s CE. Gladiator games truly ended with the fall of the Roman Empire in 476 CE.

Modern Gladiators

As Christianity spread across the Roman Empire, Romans became less interested in gladiator games. We no longer have gladiators today. But we still have plenty of violent sports with thousands of fans. Athletes in sports such as boxing and ultimate fighting try to hurt their opponents. They often draw blood. Sometimes they knock each other out. Like the Romans, we watch all of these sports as entertainment.

Gladiators have also found their way into popular culture. These long-gone fighters have been the subjects of popular movies like *Spartacus* and *Gladiator*. More recently, Suzanne

Banning the Games

By 400 CE, many people in the Roman Empire opposed gladiator combat. One of these people was a monk named Telemachus. In 404 CE, he ran into an arena and prevented two gladiators from fighting. The crowd was furious with Telemachus. They grabbed the monk and ripped off his limbs. Telemachus's death was so horrible that Emperor Honorius declared a ban on gladiator games.

In the book and 2012 film version of *The Hunger Games*, Katniss Everdeen enters a competition similar to ancient gladiator games to save her sister's life.

Collins's book *The Hunger Games* was made into a hit movie starring Jennifer Lawrence. The story features an event similar to ancient gladiator matches. Gladiator events may have ended more than 1,500 years ago, but people remain fascinated by gladiators to this day.

In 325 CE, Emperor Constantine issued a law called the Theodosian Code. In it he declared that the gladiator games were to be ended:

> In an age of public peace and domestic tranquility, spectacles involving the shedding of blood displease us. We therefore utterly forbid the existence of gladiators; ensure that those persons who, because of their crimes, used to be sentenced to become gladiators, should now be sentenced to the mines, so that they can pay the penalty for their criminal behavior without having to shed their blood.
>
> Source: Alan Baker. The Gladiator: The Secret History of Rome's Warrior Slaves. New York: Thomas Dunne, 2000. Print. 198.

Nice View

Reread Tertullian's quote from Chapter Five. Think about the similarities and differences between Tertullian's point of view and Emperor Constantine's point of view. How are these two points of view similar? How are these points of view different? Write a short essay that answers these questions.

IMPORTANT DATES

500 BCE

Romans conquer the Italian peninsula.

200s BCE

Gladiator games begin appearing at funerals.

100s BCE

Gladiators begin fighting in arenas.

325 CE

Emperor Constantine temporarily bans gladiator games.

399 CE

Gladiator schools are banned, and the final school is shut down.

404 CE

The monk Telemachus runs into a Roman arena to protest a gladiator fight. The crowd kills him.

73 BCE

Spartacus leads a gladiator rebellion.

44 BCE

Julius Caesar's funeral includes 300 pairs of gladiators.

27 BCE

Augustus becomes the first Roman Emperor, officially founding the Roman Empire.

404 CE

Emperor Honorius declares another ban on gladiator games.

440s CE

Gladiatorial combat is still written about, though the games have been officially banned.

476 CE

The Roman Empire ends, also ending gladiator games.

Dig Deeper

What questions do you still have about gladiators? Do you want to learn more about their weapons? Or their fighting techniques? Write down one or two questions that can guide you in doing research. With an adult's help, find a few reliable new sources about gladiators that can help answer your questions. Write a few sentences about how you did your research and what you learned from it.

You Are There

Imagine you are a gladiator living in the Roman Empire. Write 300 words describing your life. What does your cell look like? How does the food taste? What weapons do you fight with? Are you afraid? Tired? Determined? Why are you there? Are you a slave, a war prisoner, or a volunteer?

Why Do I Care?

Roman gladiators may have lived 2,000 years ago, but their lives aren't completely different from our lives today. Have you ever done something in front of a large group of people? Write a short essay about how this book connects to your life.

Take a Stand

This book discusses how exciting people found the gladiator contests to be. If you were in the audience, do you think you would have been excited too? Write a short essay explaining your opinion. Include reasons for your opinion and facts and details to support those reasons.

GLOSSARY

agile
quick and flexible

conquer
to take over an entire group of people so they have to follow the winning nation's rules and laws

despise
strongly dislike

griffin
a mythical creature that has the body of a lion and the head and wings of an eagle

invincible
unbeatable

oath
a promise to do something

opponent
a rival or enemy

plumes
featherlike decorations at the top of a helmet

specialist
someone who is an expert at something

stamina
endurance

trident
a three-pronged weapon

LEARN MORE

Books

Forward, Toby. *Gladiators*. Somerville, MA: Candlewick, 2009.

Malam, John. *You Wouldn't Want To Be a Roman Gladiator*. New York: Franklin Watts, 2000.

Mann, Elizabeth. *The Roman Colosseum*. New York: Mikaya Press, 1998.

Web Links

To learn more about gladiators, visit ABDO Publishing Company online at **www.abdopublishing.com**. Web sites about gladiators are featured on our Book Links page. These links are routinely monitored and updated to provide the most current information available.

Visit **www.mycorelibrary.com** for free additional tools for teachers and students.

INDEX

ABOUT THE AUTHOR

Paul Hoblin has a master of fine arts in creative writing from the University of Minnesota. He has written several books for children.